Golden Fleece Australia Pty Ltd - ACN 113 661 608
PO Box 2133, Tuggeranong ACT 2901, Australia
www.golden-fleece-australia.com.au
mythology@golden-fleece-australia.com.au
mythology@golden-fleece-international.com.au

ISBN   978-0-9943771-6-6

Phone/Fax: +61 2 6287 4554
Mobile   : +61 4 2235 2433

The Adventures of Daedalus & Icarus

Written by Mary Maria Papaoulakis

Illustrated by Eduardo Enrique Compdepadros

About 3000 years ago close to the Acropolis Temple, there was a market where many sculptors and architects used to create beautiful work. One of the most famous architects was Daedalus and his son Icarus. Daedalus' work was outstanding and many of his colleagues would whisper that Athena the goddess and Hephaestus the god of fire had given Daedalus a rare gift. Daedalus was famous throughout Greece, Egypt, and even in Persia.

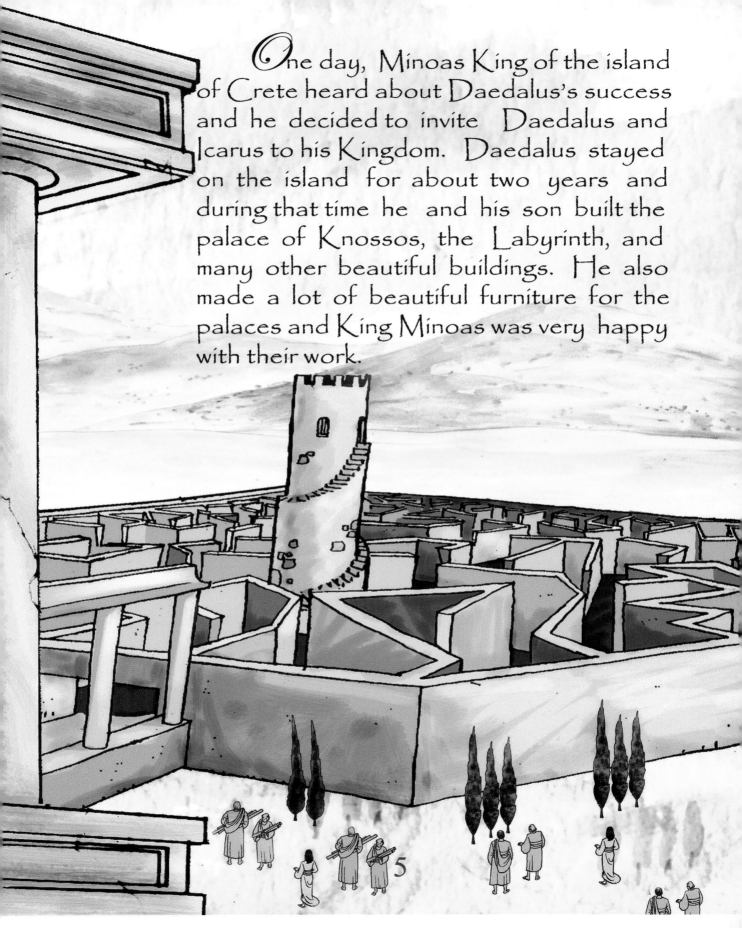

One day, Minoas King of the island of Crete heard about Daedalus's success and he decided to invite Daedalus and Icarus to his Kingdom. Daedalus stayed on the island for about two years and during that time he and his son built the palace of Knossos, the Labyrinth, and many other beautiful buildings. He also made a lot of beautiful furniture for the palaces and King Minoas was very happy with their work.

5

When Daedalus and Icarus had finished their work Daedalus told King Minoas that he wanted to return to Athens. However, the King became furious and overcome with jealousy because he was afraid that Daedalus and his son Icarus might build buildings just like the Labyrinth, so he refused to let them go. He ordered the guards to take them into the Labyrinth.

Daedalus and Icarus were unable to go against the decision of the king Minoas, they accepted their unfortunate fate to go to the prison.

10

While Icarus was spending his days with frustration in the prison, thinking all the time how to escape, particularly that the king Minoas heavily guarded the land and the sea in the island.

Icarus most of the time was trying to discuss the matter with his father, but Daedalus had no favourable answer for his son to satisfy him, until one day.....

While Daedalus was watching the sky from the small window of the prison, he saw how the birds are flying happily, he said to his son "I found it", you should not be worry any more, we have to make wings to fly like those birds.

13

When Queen Passefai heard about King Minoas's unfair decision she paid a visit to Daedalus and Icarus. Daedalus asked Queen Passefai to help them by bringing them feathers from birds.

Daedalus and his son each made a pair of wings that they could strap to their arms. The quills were threaded to a frame but the smaller feathers were held together by bees-wax.

When the wings were ready Daedalus said to his son: "Be careful my son! Please don't fly close to the sun." Icarus said: "Don't worry father I'll be careful.

19

Unfortunately, the trip was so pleasant that they felt like birds and like any other child Icarus ignored his father's warning and was thrilled by the power of flight. Icarus flew higher and higher towards the sun. Suddenly, the wax of his wings melted and Icarus fell into the deep water of the sea and drowned.

Since then, the island was called Icaria and the sea Icaria Pelagos in memory of his son. Daedalus continued his trip in deep sorrow till he reached the island of Sicily where he lived the rest of his life. Daedalus and his son Icarus were the first men to fly.

20489534R00016

Printed in Great Britain
by Amazon